James Kelly

Inspiration: A dialogue between a Christian and his pastor

James Kelly

Inspiration: A dialogue between a Christian and his pastor

ISBN/EAN: 9783337198077

Printed in Europe, USA, Canada, Australia, Japan

Cover: Foto ©Lupo / pixelio.de

More available books at **www.hansebooks.com**

INSPIRATION;

A DIALOGUE BETWEEN A CHRISTIAN AND HIS PASTOR.

BY THE REV. JAMES KELLY, M.A.,

AUTHOR OF "THE ETERNAL PURPOSE OF GOD,"
"THE APOCALYPSE INTERPRETED IN THE LIGHT OF
'THE DAY OF THE LORD,'" &c., &c.

LONDON:

JAMES NISBET AND CO.,

BERNERS STREET.

—

1862.

PRICE ONE SHILLING.

CONTENTS.

INSPIRATION;

A DIALOGUE BETWEEN A CHRISTIAN AND HIS PASTOR.

Christian. I am truly glad to have this opportunity of conversing with you. And if you allow me, I should like to turn it to account, by eliciting from you some clear and definite view of Inspiration.

Pastor. I am not surprised to find that your attention has been arrested to this subject. My own mind has been much exercised on it of late. Indeed, I trust that the spirit of inquiry which has been awakened on the point amongst God's children generally, will prove to be one good educed from the evil of those obnoxious Essays of which we have heard so much.

Christian. I must confess what has harassed me most, has been, not so much the allegations of these gainsayers of the truth, as the suicidal principles put forth by some of our late writers on the evidences, and the equivocalness of some of our leading Evangelical ministers.

Pastor. I suppose by way of not committing themselves to what they call an untenable position, they have made what you consider dangerous concessions ?

Christian. That may be. I question not the
motives, but the concessions are of such a kind,
that really I can't see how, by those who make
them, any portion of Scripture can be vindicated
as the Word of God.

First of all, verbal inspiration is abandoned.
Then the matter of the Bible, as regards the
physical facts related.   Then its historical facts,
as bearing on what is called profane history.
Then even its own proper history ; and lastly, the
reasoning of the inspired writers.   Such is the
surrender of the truth which has been made by
living authors, even Bishops in our Church.*   Is

* " With the gradual progress of enquiry, however, and
the more diligent use of Scripture, a further limitation
came in time to be put on Scriptural Inspiration. It
became a question whether even all the *matter* of the Bible
was to be considered as having the stamp of Divine truth
upon it. The progress of natural philosophy made it impossible that any thing but blind superstition should assert
this character for all physical facts ; and the whole branch
of topics which fall under that head, have been accordingly
excluded by a great part of Christians.........But one
portion of the matter of the Bible—its natural philosophy—
having been once excluded from the sphere of Inspiration,
in the view of so many learned and pious Christians, further
doubts, on similar grounds, have been suggested respecting
the statement of those historical facts which belong not to
sacred but to profane history. It has been justly contended
that similar difficulties are obviated by excluding profane
history, as by excluding natural philosophy.

" ....The following may perhaps, on reflection, be

it any wonder that after such surrender, we should have that unblushing volume of Essays and Reviews to which you have alluded, scattering Infidelity over the land.

found not inconsistent with the purest view of God's written Word.

" It may be fairly questioned then, first, whether even its *sacred* history is inspired. For although wherever a point of faith or practice is involved in the historical record, inspiration must be supposed, (else the application of the record as an infallible rule must be abandoned,) yet, when this is not the case, there seems to be no necessity for supposing inspiration; and by not supposing it, several difficulties in the attempt to harmonize the sacred historians are removed.

" Again, proceeding still on the principle that the truth to be believed—the material of faith—is the point to which the control, or suggestions of inspiration must have been directed, and to which alone it is necessary for constituting the Bible the rule of faith, that it should be directed, the reasoning of the inspired writers may be considered safely as their own."—*Bishop Hinds.*

" ......Where the Apostles treat of the common occurrences of life and such things as have no relation to divine truths, they were not inspired. As when St. Paul speaks of his design to take Rome in his way to Spain, and to call at Corinth as he went into Macedonia, but yet it appears he was uncertain as to that resolution, and did not actually make it good. Hither, too, we may refer slips of memory in matters of no consequence, some of which there are to be found in the New Testament. Another instance, wherein we may reasonably suppose the Apostles spoke without Inspiration is, when they discourse of such things as our Saviour told them they must be content to be ignorant of.

6

Pastor. These are certainly flagrant sentiments to put forth ; and I recognize the writers to whom you allude. But you were disturbed also, you said, by the sentiments of Evangelical ministers?

Christian. Yes, and with all respect to them, I think they have for a long season unwittingly strengthened the hand of the enemy. Even the lamented Daniel Wilson, late Bishop of Calcutta, in his lectures on the Evidences of Christianity, admits *degrees* of Inspiration. He expresses himself thus :—" The prophetical parts, the doctrines of pure revelation, the historical facts beyond the

In these cases, I think it will be no prejudice to the Divine Inspiration of the Apostles, to allow them to have spoken like men."—*Bishop Lowth.*

" In matters unconnected with religion, such as points of history or natural philosophy, a writer who professes (as the Apostles do) to be communicating a Divine Revelation, imparted through him by the means of miracles, may be as liable to error as other men, without any disparagement to his pretensions; but if we reject, as false, any part of the religion which he professes himself Divinely sent to teach, we cannot consistently believe but that his pretensions are either an imposture or a delusion, and that he is wholly unworthy of credit."—*Archbishop Whateley.*

" As the more rigid theory of Inspiration was abandoned by the learned on account of the insuperable difficulties opposed to it by the discrepancies found in the Gospels, so these same discrepancies compel us to admit that the superintending control of the Spirit was not exerted to exempt the Sacred Writers altogether from errors and inadvertencies."—*Bishop of St. David's.*

reach of human knowledge, all the great outlines of Christianity, both as to doctrine and practice, were probably of the inspiration of suggestion, both as to the matter and the words, (for we think in words). Where the usual means of information, or the efforts of memory were enough, as in most of the Gospels and Acts, the inspiration of direction may be supposed to have sufficed. When the exposition of duty, or the rebuke of error, or exhortation to growth in grace, was the subject, the inspiration of elevation and strength may be considered as afforded. When matters more incidental occur, the inspiration, still lessening with the necessity, was probably that of superintendency only, preserving from all improprieties which might diminish the effect of the whole, and providing for inferior but not unimportant points of instruction. Even the slightest allusions to proverbial sayings, to the works of nature, to history, were possibly not entirely out of the range of the watchful guardianship of the Holy Spirit."

Again, "Where nature ended, and inspiration began, it is not for man to say."

The purely human theory of inspiration set forth here, making it to vary with man's estimate of the important—in other words, subjecting it to his " verifying faculty," is obvious.

And other good men, contemporaries of the Bishop, belonging to other sections of the Church, such as the late Dr. Pye Smith and Dr. Dick, have published similar views. But even living champions of the truth, whom the present exigency has drawn forth, men esteemed for piety and talent, have adopted an equivocal and hesitating tone which embarrasses the subject.

The full, plenary inspiration which extends to the minutest *words* of Scripture is called by one, the mechanical theory,* and dismissed accordingly, as though those who hold this view, regard the inspired writers as mere unsympathising machines ; whereas their position is, as it has been well put, that " In inspiration the human mind is imbued with the Divine truth ; the human feelings with the Divine affections ; the human memory furnished with the facts selected by the Divine wisdom ; that the Spirit of God is present in the thoughts, the sentiments, the faculties of the man ; and that if that man's words are saturated with the Holy Spirit, it is because in the first place, his mind and his heart have been saturated with the same Spirit."† Thus the human agent does not contribute only " the pen of the scribe," as Dr. Lee has it ; but as Hooker says, while " they (the sacred writers) neither spake nor wrote any word of their own, but uttered syllable by syllable as the Spirit put it into their mouths, no otherwise than the harp or the lute doth give a sound according to the discretion of his hands that holdeth and

* Lee on Inspiration.
† Three Discourses by A. J. Scott, M.A.

striketh it with skill," yet " herein (and Dr. Lee does not quote this) they were not like harps or lutes, but they felt the power and strength of their own words. When they spake of our peace, every corner of their hearts was filled with joy. When they prophesied of mournings, lamentations, and woes to fall upon us, they wept in the bitterness and indignation of spirit, the arm of the Lord being mighty and strong upon them."*

Another, the excellent Dr. Miller of Birmingham, demurring to the deliverance of Hooker, says, " To go to the full extent of Hooker's words, seems to invest the Original Autographs with a specialty which makes their loss irreparable, and versions and translations of painfully inferior value."†

Hence, (for this is plainly implied,) in order that we may be the better reconciled to our Bible as we have it, we are not to maintain the perfection of the original as it came from the Inspired Writers! But looking at the matter even in this practical aspect, as it has been called, surely the reflection, by a copy or translation, (however imperfect,) of a *perfect* original, is a more precious possession, than such reflection of an *imperfect* original. The deduction to be made in both cases, may be pronounced to be a common quantity. But the remainder left, must be esti-

* Hooker on Jude.
† " Bible Inspiration Vindicated," p. 37.

mated as of the quality of the original, perfect if that original be perfect, imperfect if that original be imperfect.

Once more, Mr. Birks, noted for his acuteness as a reasoner, having alluded to flaws in the Scriptures, arising from variations of copies and translations, thus continues, " There seems therefore no abstract or doctrinal objection to the admission of similar flaws in the Apostolic and Prophetical Autographs themselves. A distinction may thus be drawn between plenary inspiration in the looser sense, which claims the authority of God for every book and passage of Scripture; and verbal inspiration, which extends the principle to every separate word, and implies that the first Autographs were entirely free from verbal oversights and errors, either in number or in name."*

* "Modern Rationalism," pp. 111, 112. With the sincerest pleasure, whilst this is passing through the press, I observe that in a more recent publication, " *The Bible and Modern Thought,*" Mr. Birks expresses different sentiments. They are here subjoined, and the perusal of them will be a relief to many who have been wont to put confidence in Mr. Birks as a faithful upholder of the truth in these perilous times.

"They," (the Saviour and His Apostles,) "do not require us to believe that these messages are absolutely perfect, without the least speck or flaw, in the form in which they reach the hands of every individual, after translation and transcription have been at work for thousands of years. They do not, perhaps, require us to decide

To the same effect, Mr. Birks had said before, " Whether their writings, as they proceeded from the several authors, were free from the least manual error or lapse of memory, such as copyists and translators have introduced into later manuscripts or modern Bibles, is a more delicate question, and happily not essential to the practical maintenance of a Plenary Inspiration......It is enough to satisfy most of the above declarations, and to secure the main practical object of Inspiration, if we believe that every book, and chapter, and clause of the Bible is truly a message from God, and reveals either facts or doctrines, which it is important, though in various degrees, for the Church to know and believe ; and that if human errors have been allowed to ~enter the

how near to the fountain-head some minute, microscopical faults from the infirmity of copyists or amanuenses, may have been permitted to come. But they do seem clearly to imply that the gift was perfect, and free from all error, as first communicated from the God of truth to His chosen messengers, or curiously and wisely fashioned, by the use of their faculties, within their minds, whether in history, precept, or doctrine, devotion, or spiritual meditation. The whole, therefore, comes to us, plainly stamped with a Divine authority. And this authority must extend to every jot or tittle of its contents, until some adequate evidence, external or internal, shows it to be a fault of translation or transmission, a slight flaw, in whatever way occasioned, which has become attached to the original and Divinely perfect message."—" *The Bible and Modern Thought.*" By the Rev. T. R. Birks. London : Religious Tract Society.

Autographs, as they certainly have in copies and translations, they are both slight in amount, and separable by a due comparison of the Scriptures themselves. For instance, if St. Matthew himself, by a permitted lapse of memory, referred to Jeremiah the prediction which really belongs to Zechariah, the admission of such an oversight need involve no hazard to the faith of Christians, and does not sensibly affect, for any practical purpose, the doctrine of Plenary Inspiration; because a simple reference to the Old Testament canon serves to rectify the error. But if we hold that the Prophecy itself was misapplied, we undermine altogether his Apostolic authority as an Inspired Messenger of God, and launch on a sea of uncertainties where neither chart nor compass can be found." (Pp. 167, 168.)

Now it appears to me that Mr. Birks' consciousness of dialectical ability to thread his way amidst distinctions embarrassing to ordinary minds, has here tempted him altogether out of his depth, in fact into that very sea of uncertainty of which he admonishes his readers.

Pastor. Well. We are not to forget the importance of careful discrimination in dealing with such a subject as the Inspiration of Scripture, especially when acute minds, as in our day, are ready to take advantage of any unguarded statement. And certainly, my observation has been that it is in confounding things that differ that gainsayers make an impression. But with every desire to appreciate these distinctions of Mr. Birks', I must say that I consider them futile and dangerous.

1. Futile, for if by "Divine permission," a lapse of *memory* be assignable to Matthew, why not a lapse of *judgment* ? Where is the difference? If the one could be corrected by the *record* of the Spirit elsewhere, why not the other be corrected by the *teaching* of the Spirit elsewhere. And if there be a contradiction between the statements of Scripture, so that one is to be received and the other rejected, who is to be the arbiter?

2. The distinction is dangerous. To recognise this, we have only to remember how it has been employed by the late Dr. Arnold. Referring to the Inspiration of St. Paul, he says " Yet this great Apostle expected that the world would come to an end in the generation then existing. . . . . .Shall we say then that St. Paul entertained and expressed a belief which the event did not verify ? We may say so, safely, and reverently in this instance : for here he was most certainly speaking as a man, and not by revelation ; as it has been providentially ordered that our Lord's express words on this point have been recorded."[*] (Matt. xxiv. 36.) This also, be it added, is the stock argument of our Rationalistic Writers, and to the same end, impugning the Inspiration of

[*] " Sermons on the Christian Life, its Course," &c.

Paul's Epistles. Professor Jowett urges it in his Expository volumes, and again in the volume of Essays and Reviews.

Now if we allow that Paul could be mistaken, (and why not Paul as well as Matthew?) where are such surmises to stop? Let any passage of Scripture perplex us, and we have thus a ready way of disposing of it. We have only to argue from our ignorance, defaming as uninspired, and discarding, whatever proposition we cannot at once reconcile with our imperfect systems of Theology. Besides, how inimical this procedure to the discernment of truth! For, not to go further than the example before us of Dr. Arnold; with his notion that Paul's teaching was not infallible, all stimulus, it is obvious, was wanting to search for a reconciliation between the Apostle's words, and our Lord's. Repudiation of the former was the easy course, and it was taken; just as Luther repudiated the whole Epistle of James, because he could not at once square it with his doctrinal view of justification. Only *he* was consistent in excluding such epistle altogether from the canon of Scripture; whereas Dr. Arnold and his disciples are capricious, admitting and denying Inspiration within the compass of the same book, and even chapter, of the sacred volume.

Christian. Your citation from Dr. Arnold clearly illustrates, I conceive, the tendency of such a line of argument as Mr. Birks'. But touching the subject of the Lord's coming, as inculcated by St. Paul, and at which Dr. Arnold stumbles, alleging it to be inconsistent with Matt. xxiv. 36, what would you say is the right answer for the child of God to give?

Pastor. Before indicating the suitable answer, I think we ought to apprehend clearly, if possible, the precise discrepancy which Dr. Arnold alleges. He indeed expresses himself so obscurely on the point, that we might fail to determine it, had we it not enlarged on by others, Professor Jowett to wit.

The case, then, of these writers is this—

1. That in 1 Thess. iv. 16, 17, St. Paul inculcates the imminence of the Second Advent to be such, that he and that generation of believers to whom he wrote, might survive to be partakers of its glory, thus (it is said) in a measure, defining the time of that great event; whilst in the Gospel, our Lord insists that no man knew the time. "But of that day and that hour knoweth no man, no, not the angels which are in heaven, neither the Son, but the Father." (Mark xiii. 32.)

2. Again, it is contended that as the Second Advent did *not* occur within the Apostle's defined time, his mistake is obvious; and as compared with his assurance expressed elsewhere, (2 Tim. iv. 6,) that the time of his departure, i.e., his death, was at hand, such mistake assumes the aspect of a

downright contradiction. • Now the answer I should say is this—

1. In regard to the Apostle's teaching, 1 Thess. iv. 13—17, he simply speaks of the Lord's coming —the hope of the Church—as a suspended event over that generation to which he belonged, as it has been over every generation since. And this is the Scriptural way in which the event should always be regarded. We know not when it may transpire. We know not when it may not transpire.

2. Whereas the Apostle afterwards in his Epistle to Timothy, communicates his departure by death before the Lord's coming, as the event which awaited him, how obvious the consideration that this was the result of a *further* revelation to him ; just as Peter's similar prospect of his approaching death was indicated to him of the Lord. (2 Peter i. 15.) Thus there is no mistake corrected, or former statement contradicted, only the Divine information rendered more specific concerning one believer.

3. Then as to our Lord's utterance, whilst its import is not opposed to, yet neither is it to be confounded with the teaching of the Apostle. The Apostle's reference is to the phase of the Lord's coming in which the saints of this dispensation are *personally* interested when they shall be caught up to meet Him in the air. Our Lord speaks of His actual coming to the earth (the in-

terval, let me observe, being of a duration not sufficiently recognized by Christians) when Jerusalem and her children shall pass through the Refiner's judgment, as also the nations of the earth, prior to the establishment of Messiah's promised kingdom. The feature which is common to *both* prospects, and wherein the comparison lies, is the reserve of Divine Revelation as to the precise moment of their realization. The Church knows not when the Lord will wind up this dispensation by coming *for* His saints. Jewish disciples, called afterwards to wait for their nation's hope, the kingdom, shall not know when *with* His saints He comes to the earth. Thus the weighing the words of each Scripture leads to an acquaintance with the manifold wisdom of God; and the very variations of expression which man would get rid of as inconvenient to his harmonizing processes, are fraught with blessed instruction to the child of God.

Christian. This brings us back, then, to the point whence we started—the right view of Inspiration. For, such minute discrimination of Scripture as you have now exemplified, is what has impressed me so strongly with the sacredness of its every word. Indeed, in all your expositions of Scripture, I have observed you to compare and argue from *words,* and frequently you have shown that the key to a whole context has been found in one word. You have honoured the Scriptures as plenarily inspired, and they have seemed to disclose their treasures accordingly. Would that in the ministry of the Word, generally, the true doctrine of Inspiration were more commended to our Christian congregations by this practical exhibition of its use. But now, will you give me a clear and digested view on the subject, that I may not only be satisfied myself, but be helpful to others in conversing upon it.

Pastor. By all means, I shall endeavour to respond to your wishes ; and may the unction that is from above, anoint the eyes of our understanding, and give us a right judgment on the occasion !

First, then, I would observe, let us make the *Word* itself our sole standard of authority. What do the Scriptures say of themselves ? Let us not argue from any view of ours antecedently, as to the necessity of the case, which is the course I see sometimes taken, *but from what God affirms is the case.* For, as in regard to the *contents* of revelation, we are not, as Bishop Butler insists, competent to determine beforehand what these should be ; so in regard to the manner and measure of the Spirit's working. How far He has intervened in the giving of that Revelation, can alone be ascertained from His own teaching. Of course, in saying this, I contemplate that I am speaking to one who receives the Bible as the Word of God, but who seeks to determine what it teaches on this, as on any other doctrine. Were it otherwise,

and I were dealing with a Deist, it is obvious that
another line should be pursued. I should have to
prove that the Bible was a revelation from God,
i.e., *a standard of appeal;* and not till then, could
I argue its *exactness* as a standard. But with the
believer, with you and Christian brethren, I
assume only common ground. We all hold the
Bible to be the Word of God, and our object is to
ascertain from the character of its own statements,
how entirely it is so.

Christian. You state the case just as I could
wish. What I covet to have elucidated, is the
perfection of the Scriptures, as God's communication of truth to man, on *every* subject on which
they treat. The commendation of the sacred
volume by Locke, as " having God for its author,
salvation for its end, and truth without any mixture of error for its matter," especially this last
clause, used to be regarded by me as a sort of
truism. But now I confess, in the light of modern
theories, I see its force and emphasis ; and this
position that the Scriptures are " *truth without
any mixture of error,*" appears to me to be all-
important for confession by Christians.

Pastor. Well, to proceed, all admit the Bible
to be inspired. Let us see the sense in which it is
so. The word " inspiration," or *in-breathing,* has
a general meaning in Scripture. It is employed
to denote the origin of man's rational and even
animal life. " There is a spirit in man, and the

inspiration of the Almighty giveth him understanding." (Job xxxii. 8.) Again, "the breath
(or inspiration) of the Almighty, (it is the same
word in the original,) hath given me life." (Job
xxxiii. 4.) The allusion is manifestly to God's
breathing into man at his creation, the breath of
life, (or *lives*, more literally,) whereby he became
the living soul that he is described. (Gen. ii. 7.)

But, whereas man fell, and the spirit in him, the
organ for communion with God now became car-
nalized, ceasing to perform its functions, we read
of the Holy Spirit of God operating thenceforth
unto man's spiritual renewal and illumination.
Thus the Holy Spirit is said to have striven with
the antediluvians, to have been vexed by Israel in
the wilderness. And so in contrast with them,
Caleb is recorded as being "a man in whom was
another Spirit;" and of "the Spirit which was
upon Moses," that God endowed therewith the
70 men, the elders of Israel who were to bear
with Moses the burden of the people. (Num. xi.
17.) Again, "the Spirit of the Lord spake by
me," says David, "and His word was in my
tongue." (2 Sam. xxiii. 2.)

Now, by this Spirit it was that all the Prophets were moved—"Holy men of God," as it is
said in Peter, who "spake by the Holy Ghost."
(2 Peter i. 21.) And so in the introduction to
their utterance, the formula constantly occurs,
" *Thus saith the Lord.*" Inspiration accordingly

resolves itself into a breathing into man, and the communication by man, of Divine truth. But as this communication may be by speaking and by writing, if we would estimate accurately the import of the term Inspiration, we must include in our consideration three things.

1. The knowledge inbreathed. 2. Its enunciation. 3. Its record, if it is to be preserved.

I do not think the division an accurate one which treats the mere knowledge communicated to the inspired person, as revelation, and confines the term Inspiration to its record. For such term, as its very etymology denotes, belongs as well, indeed primarily, to the process which precedes.

Christian. That is, if I understand you aright, you consider that the connection of Revelation with Inspiration, at its very first stage, ought to be observed by us?

Pastor. Yes, I mean that the knowledge, whatever it be, which is the subject matter of Revelation, should be recognized as Divinely imparted even by the Spirit of God, not intuitive or self-acquired. Of course, in some cases such knowledge may be imparted by vision, but this makes no difference. Or, fragments may have been previously possessed. Still, being adopted into God's Revelation, they are not the less OF HIM ; only the Divine mind had seen their relation to the Divine end, and selected them accordingly. This is to be carefully maintained. Its bearing upon our subject will perhaps be seen as we proceed.

Christian. Inspiration, then, you conceive, ought to be predicated of the knowledge imparted, as well as of its communication afterwards, whether orally or by writing?

Pastor. Yes, so that instead of the terminology, Revelation and Inspiration, I should propose, as more accurately suggestive of the distinctions to be observed, *Inspiration*—Inspiration *uttered*, and Inspiration *recorded*. For, Inspiration simply, we can conceive of, as material for communion between the soul and God, without any utterance following for human ears. And it is obvious, Inspiration may be uttered without being recorded. And lastly, it may be uttered and recorded, or only recorded—as in the Scriptures. In a word, there is Inspiration of the Person, Inspiration of the Utterance, and Inspiration of the Writing.

Now the Person Inspired, (the thoughts being of God,) may also be inspired to utter these thoughts, and may aver with convincing authority that he is so. But he may speak by the Holy Ghost, without averring it. And, again, he may speak with the alloy of humanity not eliminated from his utterance. This brings me to the case of Inspiration of the *Writing.* All the variety already supposed in the Inspired person's *utterance*, might, it is obvious, characterize a *written* communication. It might be, as to every word, of

God, but not positively affirmed to be so ; or it might be as to its words, of *man*, or partly, of man ; and we might be left to determine the matter as best we could. But what we find to be the fact is, that *upon Scripture, as such*, i.e., Inspiration recorded, we have the Divine seal put in the declaration, " All Scripture is given by inspiration of God," or literally, is *God-breathed.* (2 Tim. iii. 16.) It is not the Person simply, nor his utterance of which Inspiration is predicated, but that which is written, or rather that which *was* written, for we must be careful to remember that it is of Scripture as *originally given,* that the assertion is made. I note this, because of the variations in the text as it has come down to us. Of course this suggests that after all, there is a human alloy to be found in the Scriptures as we have them ; and when this occurs, (i.e., when there is a doubt as to the reading,) we are to forbear to lean upon the precise phraseology. But it is remarkable that admitting all the variations that are alleged, they are infinitesimal in their import, and the points upon which they create suspense for a moment, are found to be positively determined for us in other parts of the Word.

Christian. But then some say that in 1 Cor. vii., the Apostle Paul specifies particular precepts which he gives as from himself, and not as Inspired. How are we to answer this ? Even in an able volume of Essays vindicating the truth on

fundamental points, which I lately met with, I
observe that the author admits this allegation to
be true; only he confines it to the one passage
adduced, treating it as the exception which proves
the rule.* But ought we to understand the Apostle as intimating that he spoke even here otherwise than by Inspiration?

Pastor. I don't wonder at your putting the
question. But there is no difficulty in the reply,
if the Apostle's words are observed carefully.

On one point, the regulation of married life, he
says, "I speak this by permission, and not by
commandment," ver. 6; i.e., he communicates
here a Divine permission, not a commandment.
This is not to be questioned. Then pursuing his
instruction of married believers, he forbids the
practice of divorce. But the Lord Himself had
done this already both personally in the New, and
by His Spirit, in the Old Testament. Therefore,
the Apostle interjects, "Yet not I, but the
Lord"—the duty was ruled already. (Ver. 10.)

* "How or where is the line of demarcation to be drawn
between the fallible and the infallible; between truth and
falsehood? The Scripture itself nowhere draws it. With
one exception only—an exception which proves the rule of
its pervading claim to infallibility—where Paul acknow-
ledges himself to speak, and 'not the Lord'—with this
solitary exception, the Scripture offers no help in deciding
where God ceases, and man begins to speak with us."—
Pp. 31, 32, *Foundations. A Series of Essays, &c.* By
Rev. W. Pollock, M.A. London: Nisbet and Co.

But now, in ver. 12, referring to cases where one of the married couples continued to be heathen—cases in which the Old Testament had enjoined separation from the heathen, he adds, " *to the rest speak I, not the Lord ;*" and thus he introduces the obligation under the Christian dispensation, to maintain the marriage union as long as the unbelieving partner might consent. The tone, in fact, of the Ambassador speaking with conscious authority, runs through the whole of this language. The only disclaimer that is uttered, is that of *priority* in regard to the communication of one of the commands in question, not at all of Inspired *authority*. Nor, be it observed, is it the speaking by such authority which is affirmed presently after, as though it had been denied, but simply that there was this priority of communication in regard to the other command. As to Inspired Authority, it had underlain all that the Apostle had said, and he brings it not into the question, except at the close of the chapter, to affirm it even for what he had recommended in the way of judgment, saying significantly, as though glancing at the counter-sentiments of others who were esteemed spiritual persons, " and I *think* also that I have the Spirit of God," (ver. 40.) Most certainly the manner of communication he employs, was not designed to qualify his assertion of the fullest Inspiration. For we find him, in a following chapter of this Epistle, winding up all his detail of precepts with these remarkable words : " If any man think himself to be a prophet, or spiritual, let him acknowledge that the things that I write unto you, are the commandments of the Lord." (1 Cor. xiv. 37.)

Christian. Do you consider, then, that we may safely affirm the proposition of Hooker, that the sacred writers " neither spake nor wrote any word of their own, but uttered syllable by syllable as the Spirit put it into their mouths."

Pastor. I do, if Hooker's proposition be taken to relate, (as it does,) to what has been written, that is to the contents of Scripture. For, let us not forget, that upon *the Writing—all the Writing,* as such, the Divine sentence has been pronounced " *God-breathed,*" and error or inaccuracy is incompatible with such sentence. The only question that can arise is, What does all the Writing, or " *all Scripture* " include—in other words, What is the canon of Scripture ?

Now it is obvious that the Books of the Old Testament, as received in the Apostle's days, belong to it. To them the term *God-breathed,* as used by him, emphatically attaches. But the Books of the New Testament, of which some were then actually extant, can be shown to be also comprised under the Apostle's designation of Scripture. Thus Peter uses the expression " the other Scriptures," to designate those that were not written by his beloved brother Paul, plainly implying that what Paul did write was Scripture.

The main point is to determine the force of this word *God-breathed*. And here we have an analogy to help us, instituted by our Lord Himself, between Inspiration and Regeneration. It occurs in His dialogue with Nicodemus, as given in John iii. But we must look at it in the Greek, as our translators have, in one verse (8) arbitrarily and unaccountably changed the rendering of the word το Πνευμα, (the one Divine agent alluded to all through,) into " *the Wind*," making the comparison to be between *two agents*, instead of between two subjects of the same agency—the inspired man and the regenerate man.

It may be well to run through the dialogue from the commencement. Our Lord had insisted on the necessity of regeneration, in order to entrance into the kingdom of God, the kingdom which constituted the hope of Nicodemus and his nation. At this teaching, Nicodemus evinced his bewilderment by asking, " How can a man enter the second time into his mother's womb, and be born?" Hereupon, (ver. 4,) our Lord adds that the regeneration in question was a spiritual change, to be operated by the Spirit; and of such operation, after the manner of the Prophet's teaching, (Ezek. xxxvi. 25—27,) He adduces the cleansing element of water as a similitude: " Except a man be born of water and of the Spirit, he cannot enter into the kingdom of God." (ver. 5.) But besides this explanation, our Lord goes on to say, " the Spirit breatheth where he willeth, and thou hearest his voice, but canst not tell whence he cometh and whither he goeth. So is every one that is born of the Spirit." With the case of *Inspiration,* Nicodemus as a Jew was familiar, and now he is told that like unto it is *Regeneration.*

Christian. This emendation of our translation certainly gives an altered view of the passage, and removes an incongruity which I have always felt to attach to our Lord's winding up of His comparison, taking that comparison in the usual way, as between two agents—the wind and the Spirit. For, with this, we ought to expect His following words to be, " So is the Spirit in producing regeneration." But they run differently, " So is every one born of the Spirit ;" that is, another *subject* is spoken of, not another *agent.* Still I must say, I feel a demur to admitting your emendation, because of its taking from us the beautiful and expressive symbolism which our version sets forth between the wind and the Spirit.

Pastor. Well, I am happy to say, I can at once relieve you from your demur. For the symbolism you value is still left to you, if only you are content to have it couched in a metaphor, instead of formally expressed in a similitude. For the verb πνεῖ contains it, and the clause may read thus : " The Spirit *breatheth as the wind,* where He willeth."

Christian. This altogether removes my scruple, and I think great light is shed by your emendation on the whole passage. But what is the bearing of it on our subject of Inspiration?

Pastor. Even this, that we are taught by it that Inspiration is analogous to Regeneration, so that we may bring our information in the one case to eke out what is deficient in the other. And it is remarkable that we have a most emphatic statement in Scripture as to the *distinctiveness* of the Spirit's work in regeneration, " that which is born of the Spirit," says our Lord, " is spirit." It is totally distinct from the flesh. Accordingly, in 1 John iii. 9, we read, " Whosoever is born of God, doth not commit sin, for his seed remaineth in him ; and he cannot sin, because he is born of God ;" i.e., though sin does attach to him that is born of God, yet it is not *as born of God,* the new nature begotten by the Spirit being incapable of sin. Applying this to the case of Inspiration, we affirm then that that which is Inspired (*God-breathed*) cannot contain error. But the sacred volume, as it originally came from God, is thus inspired. Therefore there can be no error in it— no error in its recitals—no error in its doctrines. If error be found in the sacred volume, it is either the error of the various actors related, or it is an accretion foreign to it, as sin is foreign to this new nature, and to be referred to the human hands through which it has passed ; and thus the infallibility of Scripture is our true position to take.

Christian. Well, but may not our opponents allege that these human hands include the sacred penmen themselves, that to the human element in them, a proportion of error may be ascribed?

Pastor. By no means. Such notion is excluded by the fact already noticed, that upon their work (the Scriptures) after passing through their hands, the Divine seal of Inspiration has been put. Were their Persons only said to be Inspired, the case would be different. But let us not forget it is *the writing,* of which Inspiration is predicated, so that whatever error or inaccuracy may appear, must have come from some other quarter. This view, I conceive, renders our position impregnable. A Divine work (and the Scriptures are such) may bear the mark of man's sin superinduced on it. It is so with the face of nature. The volume of Creation is not as it came forth from the hand of God. Numerous are the anomalies that encounter us on every side, but we allow them not to detract from our estimate of its original condition. As they force themselves upon our notice, the word is suggested to us, " An enemy hath done this." Meanwhile, as the Apostle says, " the invisible things of God from the creation of the world are clearly seen, being understood by the things that are made, even His eternal power and God-head, so that they (men) are without excuse." (Rom. i. 20.) Amidst all the derangement which moral evil and its consequences have produced around us, the heavens still declare the glory of God, and the firmament showeth His handiwork. Even the Incarnate Word, we may say, underwent disfigurement at the hands of men. His countenance was marred more than the sons of men. It was not mere Humanity that was seen in Him, but Humanity reproached and dishonoured. Repelling features to the eye of sense were thus *fastened on* this Personal Revelation of the Divine Glory. He was aspersed also with being a transgressor. " This man," said the Jews, " is not of God, because He keepeth not the Sabbath." Yet the glory shone through it all. Nor was men's responsibility diminished in regard to it. The humiliation of the blessed Son of God only tested the spirit men were of. They who were of God, heard God's words through Him. They who were not of God, heard them not. His intercourse with men left them no cloak for their sin. So with the *Written,* analogous to the Living Word. It has come *from God* perfect and undefiled—the mirror of infallible truth. But men have handled it irreverently, and here and there, be it admitted, it shows the marks. Still its lustre shines perspicuous, and the perverseness is obvious which would identify with it, such marks, the almost necessary condition of human contact.

Christian. Let me clearly understand the analogy you have pointed to. I observe you do not take the Inspired Person, but the Inspired Writing, as answering to the Regenerate Person. Is this correct?

Pastor. I think it is. It is quite true that our Lord's words put the analogy between that which is Inspired and that which is born of God, in the case of *Persons.* But His words are in the abstract, " The Spirit breatheth where He willeth ;" and if, as we read in the other text, (2 Tim. iii. 16,) the Scripture is, *God-breathed,* surely we may include it in the comparison as well as the Inspired Person ?

Christian. Well, admitting this—since a regenerate person may and doth commit sin (who is perfect ?) why may not an Inspired Writing err ? Does not your analogy lead to this ? Excuse me if you think me dull.

Pastor. I am really glad to have the matter sifted. Don't hesitate to demur to any observation that you may consider inconclusive. But I rather apprehend that you have lost sight of my point—the distinction between an Inspired Person and an Inspired Writing. Combined with the utterance of an Inspired Person, there may issue forth something that is of his own spirit, even as acting in the flesh is incident to him that is regenerate. And if we had not an appropriation by God of the whole utterance, we should be at a loss to discriminate what was Inspired, and what not; just as obtains in certain actions of the regenerate man. But suppose that after we had heard the utterance, and while in suspense as to the completeness of its Inspiration—*its precise character*—we had a Divine announcement made to us that it was altogether *of God,* what an advantage would not this be? Now such is the advantage we possess in the declaration that " all Scripture is Inspired, or God-breathed." It is as though the Spirit had said, ' this collection of writings, sentiments and words, to which the term Scripture belongs, may be relied on, as OF GOD.'

Hence in the Scriptures (of course as they come from God) we may be said to possess a perfect standard of truth, even as in the walk of the Lord Christ, we have a perfect standard of that which is born of God. Thus the analogies we have been led to, run up into one—the Incarnate Word, and the Inspired Word.

Christian. I now perceive the force of your remarks. The regenerate person may sin, and so the inspired person may err. But as that which is born of God in the former does not and cannot sin, so that which is Inspired, or God-breathed in the latter, does not and cannot err—this is your argument?

Pastor. Precisely. Of the words of Scripture, like the words which our Lord spoke, we may say, " they are spirit, and they are life."

The element of error is not in them. They answer to that " seed of God," which, distinct from the flesh though in it, constitutes the essence of regeneration.

Christian. This brings to my mind what I have heard alleged, (and in connection with this subject, the verbal Inspiration of Scripture,) that in the proposition, " *the sword of the Spirit, which is the word of God,*" (Ephes. vi. 17,) the antecedent to the relative "*which,*" as determined by the gender in the Greek, is Spirit ; so that the proposition is, " the Spirit is the word of God." What do you think on this point? As the Greek for " word" is in this passage (ρημα) admitted to signify the precise *term* of *speech* employed, it would seem to denote, if the criticism hold, that every word in Scripture ought to be regarded as, so to speak, impregnated by the Spirit.

Pastor. I have been arrested by the text you refer to, and did think that it had a bearing upon our subject. But the criticism is not to be relied on. The fact is, the relative in the Greek is sometimes *attracted* into the same gender with the predicate following, and this disposes of the apparent anomaly. We have an example of the same usage in Ephes. i. 14. Speaking of the sealing of the Spirit, the Apostle writes, " *which is* the earnest of our inheritance." And the relative here does not correspond with the word Spirit, but with the following word " earnest."

Christian. Thanks for the correction. It is well to unlearn a mistaken impression. But again, as we are upon the proofs in detail of the Plenary Inspiration of Scripture, let me ask, are we not right in including amongst such, and in the foreground, the emphatic language of the Apostle, " which things also we speak not in the words which man's wisdom teacheth, but which the Holy Ghost teacheth, comparing spiritual things with spiritual?" (1 Cor. ii. 13.) For, I have heard it alleged, to turn the edge of this argument, that all it proves, is the verbal Inspiration of the Apostle's *utterances*, for that he says, " which things *we speak*," not, which things we *write ?*

Pastor. The passage you quote, I regard as quite relevant to the point. For it is not to be doubted that the Apostle at least *includes* in it a reference to his *written* communications, estimating, as we do ourselves, that he spoke by his pen as well as by his tongue.

And the usage of the Spirit's reference is in accordance with this. Thus in Heb. vii., having cited the fact that our Lord was descended from the tribe of Judah, the Apostle adds, " of which tribe Moses *spake* nothing concerning Priesthood." Here the *writings* of Moses are obviously alluded to.

Again, we read in John xii. 41, " These things said Esaias, when he saw His glory, and *spake* of

Him." Yet when we turn to the Prophet, what we find is simply the record of his vision.

But, at all events, the principle here comes out, that in an Inspired *utterance*, the words are of the Holy Ghost ; and why should not the same obtain in an Inspired *writing ?* It is for the gainsayer to show there is a difference.

Christian. Here again I am satisfied. But before we leave this text, let me ask you what is the distinction between λόγος, the word here used, and ῥῆμα ; for, as you are aware, of course, upon this distinction is based another demur to the position of verbal Inspiration. It has been said, for example, that λόγος relates to the *matter* only of a statement, and that we cannot argue from it, as if ῥῆμα were the term, which, it is admitted, signifies the precise diction employed.

Pastor. I have seen much that has been advanced on the strength of this criticism, and yielded to, I cannot but think, too incautiously, by the champions of the truth.

But let us consider for a moment. How can the human mind receive the sentiments which constitute the so-called *matter of a statement,* except in the clothing of words ? Do we not think in words ? Are not words the organ of thought ? A sensation, indeed, may be impressed on us, without words. But reflection upon it, to deduce any correlative truth, we cannot exercise without words. Let a man set himself to reflect, and he will see this. Suppose then that the Inspiration of a Prophet or Apostle were confined simply to a sensational impression upon his spirit, such impression being the embryo of a Divine Revelation of truth for him to communicate, it can only come to the birth in his mind by a verbalizing process, his translating the impression into the precise truth intended. And what spirit of a man can be relied on for an accurate result here? To translate accurately a sentiment out of one language into another, is an arduous, sometimes an impracticable thing, for our learned men. But what is this to the operation of arresting and conveying in language the import of a sensational impression floating in the region of mind! On the other hand, if the Inspiration produce the conception of the truth, this is tantamount to saying that it has been a verbal Inspiration; and if, hereupon, the Inspired Person be left to communicate such conception in other words, words of his own, how liable to miscarriage? Thus, then, in Inspiration the apprehension and expression of the Divine mind by the Human medium, involves the concomitant of words; and this even leaves out of sight the fact, that in many cases the Inspired Person understood not the subject matter of the communication which he conveyed.

But, of course, in reference to your question, there is a distinction intended between the terms, λόγος and ῥῆμα, as you have noticed; and I hold it

to be simply this, that λόγος denotes a discourse in its
integrity; whereas ρημα for the most part signifies
the words in detail. As Tittmann says, "*ρημα is
the word, but λόγος is the matter itself which is in
the words, the discourse, oration.*"* And, yet,
because every discourse is composed of words,
and words compose every discourse, we find the
terms used interchangeably. Thus in the same
breath in which our Lord pronounces " that every
idle word (ῥῆμα) that men shall speak, they shall
give account thereof in the day of judgment," He
adds, " For by thy words (λόγων) thou shalt be
justified; and by thy words (λόγων) thou shalt be
condemned." (Matt. xii. 36, 37.) Again, in 1 Pet.
i. 23, the proposition, " the word of God (λόγος)
which liveth and abideth for ever," is immediately
reiterated, (verse 25,) in the quotation from the
Prophet, " the word (ῥῆμα) of the Lord endureth
for ever;" and it is added, " this is the word (ῥῆμα)
which by the Gospel is preached unto you."
(ver. 25.)

Christian. This is very satisfactory. How
pleasing to find the Scriptures furnishing to us
even our canon for criticism. But in regard to
what you have said about the *conception* even
of truth involving a verbalizing process, have
we any thing in Scripture that indicates this?
It is certainly remarkable, and in keeping
with it, that the formula of the Prophet's com-

* Tittmann on the Synonyms of the Greek Testament.

munications is so often, "Thus saith the Lord."

Pastor. Yes; and in the Inspiration of the Prophets, it is continually said that "the word of God came unto them," (Jer. i. 2 ; Ezek. i. 3 ; Hos. i. 1 ; &c.) And Balaam speaks not only of God putting the word in his mouth, but of his "hearing the words of God," when he saw the visions of the Almighty. (Num. xxii. 33 ; xxiii. 5 ; xxiv. 4.)

Christian. Then, would you not say that a practical proof of all this is furnished to us in the way in which the Holy Ghost, in the New Testament, comments on the Scriptures of the Old?

Pastor. Certainly, and the attention of Christians ought to be especially directed to this point. Take the Epistle to the Hebrews as an example. In chapter i., an argument is raised upon the word "*Son.*" In chapter ii., upon the word "*all*" in the eighth Psalm. In chapter iii., upon the title "*servant,*" given to Moses. In chapter iv., upon the word "*shall,*" the sign of the future tense. In chapter v., upon the import of the name "*Melchisedek,*" and even upon the reserve of the sacred history concerning him. In chapter viii., upon the word "*new*" in the Prophet Jeremiah. In chapter x., upon the word "*will*" (the will of God) in the 40th Psalm. In chapter xii., upon the expression "*once more*" in Haggai ii. Had others words than these, respectively, been employed by the writers in the Old Testament, the arguments of the Holy Ghost, by the pen of the Apostle, could not have been sustained. For instance, in the last case adduced, if instead of the term "*once more,*" the apparently equivalent word *again,* had been employed by the Prophet, the Apostle's conclusion, it is obvious, could not have been drawn.

Christian. I confess this is the sort of proof which I desiderate above all others, and I believe, if the ministers of Christ followed the example of this Divine teaching, more generally, they would add much to the edification of the Church of God. What a volume of information, for example, is opened out to us in the very first verse of the Bible, in the words, "*without form and void,*" applied to the chaotic condition of the earth, when God proceeded to make it into a sphere of dominion for man—words which show that that chaotic condition was not its *primitive* condition, but one superinduced in the way of judgment.*

* When it is said, "In the beginning God created the heaven and the earth," verse i., we may understand this, as referring not to an inchoate but complete work of the Divine hand; that is, not to the mere origination of *matter*—but to its organization as *heaven* and earth, according, be it observed, to the precise words of the text. Then—as the sacred record adds, in another distinct proposition—"The earth was (or *became,* as we may read it, and looking

Pastor. Yes; and as putting the Divine seal upon your illustration, it is interesting to observe, that it is said in Psalm cxix. 130, " The entrance (i.e., the *portal*) of Thy word giveth light; it giveth understanding to the simple." The allusion is obviously to the information you have remarked on, in the opening of the book of Genesis. It is as though the Bible were presented to us as the great temple of Truth, pouring forth a flood of light, at its very vestibule, upon the approaching worshipper.

Let us but reflect upon the various cosmogonies of the pagan philosophers, and of our modern geologists, and we shall then appreciate the value of this simple and concise record of the Spirit of God, which is consistent with, indeed suggestive of, every ascertained fact of science, and excludes only superficial speculations:

to the analogy of Jer. iv. 23, we may add, by reason of some stroke of judgment) without form and void, (verse ii.) Indeed, the proposition of a chaotic state attaching to the earth originally is emphatically denied in the prophet Isaiah. " For thus saith the Lord, that created the heavens: God Himself that formed the earth and made it, He hath established it, *He created it not* IN VAIN," or WITHOUT FORM,—the word is the same as in Genesis. (Isaiah xlv. 18.) How long, accordingly, before it was reduced to this state, and how long it lay therein afterwards, ere Jehovah spoke it into form for *man's* occupation, as we are not informed in Scripture, so it is obvious there is nothing for the deductions of science to contradict.

Christian. How much there is to learn from comparing the words of Scripture! I thought that in that verse in the 119th Psalm, the term "entrance" signified penetration—the penetration of Divine truth into us.

Pastor. Well, that is *a* truth; the penetration of the word into us, gives us light. But *the* truth is, as I have stated. The Hebrew word (פתח) rendered entrance, invariably means door, "the *door* of the Tabernacle," gate, "*the gate* of the city."

Christian. Is there any other Scripture that you think of, wherein a like pregnancy of meaning can be shown to attach to even single words?

Pastor. Well, one passage occurs to me, and I adduce it as showing the rich spiritual enjoyment that is evolved from an apparently unimportant date, that is recorded in the history of Noah's deliverance by the ark. "The ark rested," we read, "in the seventh month, on the seventeenth day of the month, upon the mountains of Ararat." (Gen. viii. 4.) Now this seventh month, we find from Exodus xii., became the first month ecclesiastically with the Jewish people; and on the fourteenth day of that month, was the Feast of the Passover. Of this our blessed Lord partook with His disciples. On the following day, the 15th, He suffered and died. He lay in the grave that day and the following, and on the 3rd, i.e., the 17th day of the month, He rose from the dead.

Thus His resurrection was exactly synchronous with the resting of the ark on Mount Ararat. And let us remember the crisis that this latter event constituted in the experience of Noah. Until then, his salvation was only in process. For 150 days had he been carried in the ark through the wide waste of waters, his faith, we may not doubt, reposing upon God, by whose command he had entered, and whose hand had shut him in. But, at length, as the sacred vessel grounded under him, we can conceive how his faith became assured ; his anticipations of enlargement on to his natural element, the earth, becoming thenceforth ratified by his intercourse with that earth, through the agency of the gentle dove. Now he could reckon himself as virtually installed into his new inheritance.

How close the application of all this to the great work of Redemption, especially if we contemplate its aspect towards the elect Church, now gathering ? Chosen in Christ Jesus before the foundation of the world, they were taken, we may say, in the fulness of time, when His hour came, into His actual embrace of love, even as Noah was received into the Ark. Upon Him, their surety, were their sins laid ; and when He died, they died in Him. The flood of wrath was thus undergone by their glorious Head. But has He emerged from it? His last words, (it is true,) were, " IT IS FINISHED." But is it really

so ? Lo! the Divine demonstration answers,
" God hath raised Him from the dead, and given
Him glory, that your faith and hope might be in
God." (1 Peter i. 21.) And another Apostle
says : " Therefore if any man be in Christ,"
(this Christ who has died and risen again,) " he is
a new creature ; old things are passed away;
behold, all things are become new." (2 Cor. v.
17.) That is, from our vantage ground in the
risen and exalted Christ, we may look forth and
discern not only our salvation sure, but its glory
at hand. The Holy Ghost the Comforter, the
true Dove, delighting in ministering to us the
earnest of our promised inheritance. Thus an
insignificant date, as it might be regarded, becomes an index to the typical relation between
the Ark and Christ. The very day whereon it
rested on the Mount, He rose from the dead.

And, that we have a typical relation here commended to us, not an undesigned coincidence, is
abundantly plain from the expansion of the allusion by the Holy Ghost: " The like figure where-
unto even baptism doth now save us (not the
putting away the filth of the flesh, but the answer
of a good conscience towards God) by the resurrection of Jesus Christ from the dead," (1 Pet. iii.
21 ;) that is, dead and buried with Him by baptism, (for such is the import of the ordinance as
clearly taught by Paul,) we *are saved by the resurrection of Christ;* saved, as justified—actually;

saved, as glorified—in hope. The "old things," the things of the old creation, are extant to the eye of sense, but "the new things," the new Heaven and earth, fill the eye of faith. And then the Apostle blessedly adds, "and these all things (τα δε παντα) are of God, who hath reconciled us to Himself by Jesus Christ," (v. 18;) that is, this universal regeneration is of Him, who has given the earnest of it already in the salvation of the Church, the body of Christ.

Again, in that solemn obituary presented to us in Genesis v., wherein is recorded the death of the great Patriarchs of mankind, commencing with Adam, the force of a single word employed to set forth the character of one of them, opens to us a rich vein of instruction; I allude to the expression, " *walked with God*," applied to Enoch. This is generally taken to denote simply a religious life, in contrast with the course of the irreligious world. But we observe, it is not as contrasted with the irreligious, but in a line with godly Patriarchs, who in this general sense all walked with God, that Enoch here takes his place; so that according to such general view of the expression, nothing peculiar comes to be assigned to Enoch's character. This is disconcerting. Let us, however, recognize the expression in question as importing the enjoyment of the DIVINE CONFIDENCE, that is, that Enoch was the *confidant of God ;* and now his distinction above the other

Patriarchs is plain ; whilst the note of time which is added, that " he walked with God *after he begat Methuselah*," is full of meaning, as signifying the particular period when he was admitted to so great a privilege; for " *Methuselah* " is compounded of two words, " He dies, it comes ;" and it is remarkable that Methuselah's death was the precursor of the Flood. Thus his birth was the occasion of the coming judgment of the flood being confided to Enoch ; he was named accordingly ; and then ensued the distinction by which Enoch is henceforth characterized, " *He walked with God.*"

What confirms the interpretation of this expression, elicited from the context itself, is the fact that in the only other place where it occurs, (Genesis vi. 9,) it is predicated of Noah, in immediate connection with the communication to him of the same event, the coming Deluge.

Christian. How often have I overlooked in the sacred narrative what now seems so plain, the note of time, *when* Enoch walked with God! This of itself I now see ought to have arrested my attention to something more peculiar being intended than Enoch's piety. How true it is that there is no redundancy in Scripture! For every word there is a use, and our wisdom is to discover it.

In accordance with this, as it is not foreign to our point, let me ask, do you not think that something profitable for us to learn, underlies the very variations of Scripture which are fastened on by its traducers, to maintain what they call its fragmentary character. For example, the change of name in the designation of God, which occurs in the beginning of Genesis. This has been alleged, as you know, to prove what is called the documentary hypothesis, i.e., that there were several documents, legends, originally in circulation, recounting the history of creation, in some of which God (Elohim) was used, in others Jehovah (LORD), and that out of them, mingled together, the writer composed his narrative.

Pastor. All which allegations are utterly gratuitous, and only show the spirit of the men from whom they proceed. They base their reasoning on what they call philology; but it is really systematized ignorance, ignorance of the matter of Scripture, sheltered under a pretentious citation of its terms. Indeed, I quite agree with you, that what these infidels stumble at, is replete with instruction to the child of God. God (Elohim) is the comprehensive name of the Creator, the fountain and end of creaturehood. Jehovah (LORD), His title of relation to that creaturehood, sustaining and directing it, working in it unto the accomplishment of his own purpose.*

---

* After a consideration of various theories put forth by German Theologians to distinguish the import of the above names of God, *Kurtz*, in his "History of the Old Covenant,"

Accordingly with this title, as growing out of it, is constantly associated the further title of Redeemer. A digest of those ·passages of Scripture, where the two names occur, will evidence this. Let us

thus sums up the matter: " They stand in the relation of potency to evolution—of the beginning, which, in potency, already contains the entire development, to the progress, during which this potency is actually evolved in outward appearrances. *Elohim* is the God of the commencement, who in Himself has the potencies of all life and development—who by his creative agency, presents them external to Himself, and initiates the commencements of history, which are afterwards to be so fully developed. On the other hand, *Jehovah* is the *God* of *the development*, who takes up the work of Elohim, who causes the potencies to unfold, and directs what was begun to a termination.......

The name Elohim indicates absolute fulness and power of life, and assures us that every product of His activity is rich in, and capable of, development—that it *may* perfectly unfold and attain its goal, and not that it certainly shall do so. On the other hand, the name of Jehovah guarantees the development itself, and that the potency will ultimately reach its fullest development, that what was begun shall reach its proper termination. For in His character of Jehovah, God undertakes the development; it now rests upon Him, He becomes its co-efficient, and He unfolds Himself *in* and along *with* the mundane and creature development. Hence, despite the vicissitudes and disturbances caused by the co-operation of man's free will, it must necessarily reach its goal. The guarantee for the development and the attainment of the goal offered by the name יְהֹוָה is distinctly pointed out in the explanation of that name in Ex. iii. 14, by אֶהְיֶה אֲשֶׁר אֶהְיֶה .—*Kurtz' History of the Old Covenant.* Introduction, pp. 22, 23.

confine ourselves for the present to the first few
chapters in Genesis; they will sufficiently illus-
trate the point.

In chapter i., wherein the works of Creation
are described, the word employed is invariably
God (Elohim). Then, in a recapitulation—the
recital of creation work, including man in the
category ending at chapter ii. 3—occurs for the
first time, the name LORD (Jehovah), and man is
introduced again, with Eden his assigned abode,
indicating that he occupies a special place in the
Divine counsels. In chapter iii., however, (the
narrative of the Temptation,) it is observable, that
the Tempter employs not this significant name,
but only that of God (Elohim): " Yea, hath God
(Elohim) said," &c., and thrice he confines himself
to this more distant indication of the Author of their
being. Eve, also, in her answer, corrects not the
Tempter, by referring to the nearer relation in
which God stood to her and Adam. Herein, doubt-
less, had been her victory in the conflict. The
name of the Lord would have proved a strong tower
into which she had run and been safe. (Prov. xviii.
10.) But, alas! she takes up the Tempter's word,
and merely replies, " *God* (Elohim) hath said,"
(ver. 3.) The transition, however, to the name
" LORD God," (Jehovah Elohim,) is immediate,
when the Spirit describes the scene which follows,
the vain hiding of Adam and his wife from their
offended Creator. " They heard the voice of the

c

LORD God walking in the garden, and they hid
themselves from the presence of the LORD God."
And for the remainder of the chapter, which re-
counts the disclosures of Redeeming love, with its
assurance of mercy rejoicing over judgment, the
use of this Covenant name is carefully retained.
(Verses 9, 13, 14, 21, 22, 23.)

In ch. iv., also, the worship which is described,
is presented to the LORD (Jehovah); and at the
close a remarkable notice is recorded, implying
that after an interval of declension from such
worship, when the faithful separated themselves
from the evil, the name of the LORD (Jehovah)
was their rallying standard: "Then (i.e., after
Seth had his son Enos born to him) began men
to call upon the name of the LORD (Jehovah)."
(Gen. iv. 26.)

Perhaps the recurrence to the name God
(Elohim) in the next chapter, v. 1, may perplex,
after your following me so far. But all is consistent, if we only remember that that verse is
simply a note of time in regard to *Creation ;* and
though it is again introduced in the commendation of Enoch, " who walked with God,"
(Elohim,) this may well be taken as setting forth
the end to which he attained, by his following on
to know the LORD (Jehovah).

For, be it observed, Enoch was of the line of
Seth, who were distinguished, as we have seen,
by the calling upon the name of the LORD,

(Jehovah.) · He recognized the LORD, of whose
nearness to him in grace he had continued experience, *to be his God,* the fountain of his being,
the God who had made heaven and earth. And
thus Israel, and the nations subordinately to them,
shall eventually be brought to love and serve God
(Elohim). They shall learn of Him by His
name LORD (Jehovah), fully rendered out in
Jehoshuah, i.e., Jésus, and at length will love
and serve Him. Their impulsive acknowledgment
of Him of old, when for a season, under the ministry of Elijah, they turned to Him with the
penitent cry, " The LORD (Jehovah) He is the God
(Elohim); the LORD (Jehovah) He is the God
(Elohim)" (1 Kings xviii. 33,) shall eventually
become the confession of a true faith issuing from
new hearts, and they will delight in propagating
it throughout the world, calling to all lands,
" Know ye that the LORD (Jehovah) He is God
(Elohim)." (Psalm c. 3; Isaiah xxxvii. 20.)

Christian. I am truly thankful for these hints
towards investigation of the wondrous things
contained in God's word. But as you have dwelt
upon the import of the name LORD, or JEHOVAH,
may I ask, how you understand the reference to
it by God himself, in His communication with
Moses, when he says, " I am the LORD: and I
appeared unto Abraham, unto Isaac, and unto
Jacob by the name of God Almighty, but by my
name JEHOVAH was I not known to them."

(Exodus vi. 2, 3.) This appears to be at variance with the fact recorded in Gen. xv. 6, that " Abraham believed in the LORD," and again, verse 7, that God said to him, " I am the LORD" (Jehovah).

Pastor. The simple solution of the difficulty, I conceive to be this, that it is the *experimental* knowledge of Him under the name LORD (Jehovah), which God denies that the Patriarchs possessed.

Of the mighty power involved in that name, they had not had *proof* given them. But now it was to be given to their descendants, in their redemption with a strong hand from their bondage to Pharaoh. Accordingly, God presently declares, " The Egyptians shall know that I am the LORD (Jehovah), when I stretch forth my hand upon Egypt." (Exodus vii. 5.) What remarkably confirms this explanation as the correct one, is the emphatic statement in the Psalms, " The LORD (Jehovah) is known by the judgment which He executeth." (Psalm ix. 16.)

But now, with your leave, as you seem to care for suggestive remarks to promote searching of the Scriptures, I pass on to another example of Rationalists, as they call themselves, stumbling at the Divine wisdom. I refer to the objection taken by them to the variations in the Gospels.

Christian. I covet very much indeed to hear something on this point. But before you go into it, let me observe that I have lately heard it propounded in support of *degrees* of Inspiration, that the Gospels, as records of facts and incidents for the most part naturally known to the writers, required not the same amount of inspiration as other Scriptures, i.e., the Prophecies, and the Epistles. How is this position to be met?

Pastor. 1. Generally, I should say, by the denial that there are degrees of inspiration, more than degrees of creative power. The flower beneath our feet, and the planet that rolls over our head, are alike the fruit of the latter, and *all Scripture* is alike the fruit of the former. Who can measure the Infinite, so as to assign to it a graduated scale! The idea is as unphilosophical as it is irreverent.

2. It is not simply because the events occurred, that they are recorded in Scripture, but because they were all elements in the Divine purpose of self-manifestation. " These things," says the Apostle, " happened unto them for ensamples, (types τυποὶ) and were written for our admonition." (1 Cor. x. 11.) Thus every incident related in the Bible, has been *selected* by God for His purpose of revelation ; the most simple as well as the most complicated.

3. In regard to the Gospels, innumerable are the incidents which might have been recorded concerning our blessed Lord : " There are also many other things," says John, " which Jesus did, the which, if they should be written every

one, I suppose that even the world itself could
not contain the books that should be written."
(John xxi. 25.) Again, "Many other signs truly
did Jesus, in the presence of His disciples, which
are not written in this book." But there was one
glorious theme which determined the inclusion of
whatever has been written, and so the Evangelist
adds, with emphasis : " But these are written, that
ye might believe that Jesus is the Christ, the Son
of God ; and that believing ye might have life
through His name." (John xx. 30, 31.) The question hereupon occurs, Who, for the setting of it
forth, was adequately acquainted with that glorious
theme ? And the answer is at hand : " No man
knoweth the Son, but the Father." (Matt. xi. 27.)
What but infinite wisdom could have guided in
the construction of such a biography ? It was not
merely that the sayings, and doings, and sufferings,
of Emmanuel, had to be collected before the mind's
eye of the Evangelists ; but they had to be
distributed under their appropriate heads, and
even the Divine agency narrated, which operated
unto His birth, rested on Him throughout His
life, and sustained Him in His mysterious death.
The vail of eternity had to be penetrated to
give an account of Him " whose goings forth were
of old from everlasting," but who at length had
become the babe of Bethlehem. The portraiture
required had to combine the ideal of the sublimest
power with that of the tenderest compassion, to

depict Him of whom it is written, "He telleth the number of the stars ; He calleth them all by their names;" and again, "He healeth the broken in heart, and bindeth up their wounds." (Psalm cxlvii. 3, 4.)

4. As to the observation and memory of the Evangelists sufficing to the record of the facts which they witnessed, so that for such record, a plenary inspiration was not required, the reply is obvious. Something of material of this kind, was possessed by every inspired writer. Thus, Moses giving an account of the process of creation, had the works of that creation around him ; he had grown up amidst them. Isaiah, also, and all the Prophets who foretold the future, were familiar with the events of their own day—the starting points whence that future branched forth. (See Isaiah vii.) The inspiration of these holy men of God, in regard to all such *material*, lay in the illumination cast upon it by God, so that its secret springs and relations were laid bare by them. Be it admitted, then, that to the Evangelists who companied with our blessed Lord, there necessarily accrued a knowledge of many of His words and actions ; that they stood observant before that blessed one, the Head of the new creation, as he pursued His career of redeeming love; how did all this abate the *needs be* of the fullest inspiration, to enable them to set forth their great subject, without misconception, inaccuracy, or confusion ; yea, (for herein

lies the unique character of the Gospels,) so as to suggest to the reader, the very current of their blessed Master's feelings, the manifold associations of His thoughts?

5. But, further, it is manifest that no such economy of inspiration as that suggested, was employed of God; for we find one Evangelist relating, not what he, but the other, saw. For example, Matthew witnessed neither the Transfiguration on the Mount, nor the agony of our Lord in Gethsemane, and yet he records these scenes, giving even the words that were spoken, as also do Mark and Luke; whilst John, who was present on both occasions, omits all mention of them.

6. The simple fact is, and this brings me back to the point I was on—To each Evangelist, underlying his consciousness, how much soever, of free agency, was assigned of God, his peculiar department in the composition of the exquisite Mosaic of the Gospels; and the matter was distributed accordingly. That line of narrative which belonged to the design of the Spirit in one Gospel, was kept distinct from the lines drawn in others; whilst all converged to their focus in the one glorious subject, so that the omissions of the Evangelists, respectively, are but the subtle shadings of the great Artist, full of wisdom for us to study.

Christian. I have often considered that, as you

observe, there must be a peculiarity attaching to each Gospel. But don't you think that the prevailing disposition to harmonize the Gospels, has tended to obscure the recognition of this?

Pastor. Quite so, and perhaps we may add that the industry in such direction, of our Har-. monists, has arisen from their having in view the refutation of Infidels, rather than the edification of the Church of God. But they ought to have remembered that in the Gospels, as in all the Scriptures, the latter was the primary object of the Holy Ghost, and that in the discernment of the same, lies the truest improvement of our blessing. It is when we understand what the Great Teacher says to ourselves as disciples, that we are best qualified to answer the gainsayer. Surely it ought to have occurred to the writers in question, that if it were the design of the Holy Ghost to give us one condensed history of our blessed Lord, He could have done so. But in that He has given us *four* instead, we must miss His end, if, no matter for what object, we practically compress them into one. It is as if the student of nature would insist on reducing to white light the prismatic colors of the rainbow, rendered out for his greater admiration of the luminary above him ; and one mischief has been, that the peculiarities. of the Gospels, with the variations involved, have been treated as incongruities to be explained away, instead of characteristic traits to be reverently expounded.

Christian. What would you say, then, are the characteristics of the Gospels? I am familiar with the comparison of the Evangelists to the heads of the four orders of animated nature, the Lion, the Ox, the Man, and the Eagle. But the distribution of these symbols is different with different writers.

Pastor. The diversity you speak of has arisen, probably, from the mistake (tradition corrupting the truth) of attaching these symbols to the Evangelists *personally*, instead of to their *great subject* whom they pourtray.

It is as setting forth the Person of our blessed Lord in His manifold relations, that I conceive such symbols find their true significancy; and the index to guide us in their determination, respectively, seems furnished to us in the Gospels themselves.

For example, the Lion is the Scripture symbol for Royalty, and especially that of Messiah in connexion with the tribe of Judah; wherefore He is designated " the Lion of the tribe of Judah.' And we have only to observe the style and tenor of the Gospel by St. Matthew, to see how this aspect of *dignity* is brought out in all that is related of our blessed Lord.

· 1. His genealogy is traced up to David and Abraham; and his birth as " King of the Jews "

is announced, and proclaimed, and homage done
him accordingly.

2. The kingly air is prominent, with which He
dispenses His miraculous beneficence; likewise the
authority with which He delivers his discourses.

3. In St. Mark's Gospel, the symbol of the
patient Ox has its appropriateness: our Lord being
at once brought upon the stage, as the girded
servant, without any introduction, and pursuing
his career of doing, and teaching, as man's exi-
gencies required. Dignity is put in the back-
ground here, and the conspicuous feature is
laborious, patient, sympathizing service ; to which
also, He purports to be sent forth at the very
beginning of His ministry : " Immediately," i.e.,
after his baptism, " the Spirit driveth him into
the wilderness" to be tempted; "driveth" (ἐκβάλλει),
the same word which he employs himself when
contemplating the Lord of the Harvest, as *sending
forth* labourers into his harvest. (Matt. ix. 38 ;
Luke x. 2.)

4. Then, in Luke's Gospel, the import of the
symbol—*Man*, comes out, in the presentation of
our Lord as the Redeemer of mankind at large,
occupying a wider relation than His Jewish one,
in which Matthew exhibits Him. Accordingly,
here His genealogy is traced up beyond David and
Abraham, even to Adam.

5. Lastly, in John's Gospel, the soaring Eagle
making its nest on high, applies to the transcen-

dant dignity of the eternal Word at length made flesh, asserted in the introduction of the Evangelist, and avowed by the glorious one Himself, in not a few of His discourses which follow.

Thus the key hangs at the door, as it were, of each Gospel, whereby to open and classify its contents ; and to reverent enquiry, I am convinced every variety in the narratives will disclose itself as characteristic of some design of the Holy Ghost.

Of some artists it has been pronounced by a master critic,* that when they look at a face, they do not give it the attention necessary to discern what beauty is already in its peculiar features ; but only to see how best it may be altered into something for which they have themselves laid down the laws. Nature never unveils her beauty to such a gaze. She keeps, whatever she has done best, close sealed, until it is regarded with reverence."

Now to the defective appreciation by Harmonists, of the peculiarities of the Gospels in their fourfold Divine portraiture of our glorious Christ, this sentiment, I conceive, may be applied, *mutatis mutandis.* They have not perceived, because they have not believed in, the latent wisdom which that exquisite portraiture contains. They have contemplated it superficially, and not scrutinized its lines, and its shades of perfection.

Christian. I feel much impressed with the

* Ruskin.

importance of the view you have stated concerning the Gospels. But, as you have called it the key for classifying their contents, may I ask you briefly to apply it to some of the alleged cases of discrepancy of which we hear so much. For example, the diverse order in our Lord's temptations, as related by St. Matthew and St. Luke, and the various inscriptions over the Cross, as mentioned by all the Evangelists.

Pastor. By all means, let us try the key in these instances.

In St. Matthew, it is the exhibition of the Royal Messiah that influences the narrative. With the dominion, then, with which this was associated in our Lord's mind, what should we expect to prove the climax of his temptation when encountering Satan? Would it not be the proffer to him of that dominion, on the base condition of his doing homage to the usurper, as the bestower of it,—the very enormity of evil which is yet to characterize the Antichrist of the last days? Now the order in Matthew, which is probably the chronological one, brings out this. This constitutes the last attempt of the enemy to shake the stedfastness of our Lord.

If we look at our Lord also in his representative character in relation to His people Israel, how fit that the inordinate lust of that people after earthly ascendancy, for the attainment of which they shall at last bow the knee in abominable idolatry, should be seen confronted by His (the true Israel's) patient waiting upon Jehovah as the fountain of His looked-for honor. Hence, another ground of appreciation of the order in Matthew.

But on the other hand, turning to St. Luke's Gospel, and remembering that herein the design of the presiding Spirit is to set forth what relates to man as man, may we not discern, in the incitement to distrust of God being presented as the climax of the scene, a reference to that generic temptation which was fatal to our first parents in Eden. (Gen. iii. 13.) For, putting God to the proof as to the faithfulness of His word, distrusting Him, was, on this occasion also, the point of the Tempter's proposition.

Christian. May I interrupt for a moment, by a question which occurs to me? You make the sin to which Satan incited our Lord, when he urged Him to cast Himself down from the pinnacle of the temple, that of distrust. But was it not rather presumption, presuming upon Divine interposition when not in the path of duty? This is certainly the common impression which prevails.

Pastor. I believe such is the case, but it is not the less a mistake. In the light of our Lord's answer, "Thou shalt not tempt the Lord thy God," we clearly read its import. Thus it was a "*tempting*" of God which had been urged; and this always means in Scripture, distrusting Him. In fact, our Lord's words are taken from Deut.

vi. 16, the whole sentence being, " Ye shall not tempt the Lord your God, as ye tempted him in Massah;" and if we turn to Exodus xvii. 7, we shall see at once what it was that occurred at Massah, not an outbreak of undue confidence or presumption, but a doubting of the gracious presence of God, " Is the Lord among us or not ?"

Christian. Truly, how much we have to unlearn of conventional interpretation of Scripture ! But now, returning to the point you were on, the diverse order of the temptations as given in Matthew and Luke, you consider that this is in designed keeping with the purport of these Gospels, respectively, and I greatly appreciate the remark—still the difficulty arises, how can the events have had two different successions, unless they occurred twice ?

Pastor. True; but different successions are not ascribed to them. There was the one succession, and that seems to be given in Matthew. It is only *the order of recital* that is different, and as we have seen for a reason. In accordance with this, it is remarkable that only in Matthew have we notes of successive time introduced, " Then," " Then." In Luke the connection is simply " And," " And." And of course, it is quite conceivable that events, after being related in their chronological order with one view, may be distributed in another order, with another view.

So much, then, for the vaunted difficulty about the history of the Temptation.

Let us now apply the same key, (the characteristic purport of each Gospel,) to the variations in the inscriptions over the Cross.

Of course we need not occupy ourselves with the allegation that there is any *contradiction* in these inscriptions. For we have only to consider that the full inscription was as John has it, with the addition of the demonstrative pronoun, and the verb substantive, which occur in Matthew and Luke, " This is Jesus of Nazareth, the King of the Jews," and of course the whole proposition contains its parts. If *all* the words in question were inscribed, then *some* of them were. The only question is—and it has a value for the child of God, apart from any cavils of sceptics— Why did the Evangelists, or rather the Spirit of God by them, combine the words so variously— *Matthew* recording " This is Jesus the King of the Jews ;" *Mark*, " The King of the Jews ;" *Luke*, " This is the King of the Jews ;" *John*, " Jesus of Nazareth, the King of the Jews ?"

Now in all these inscriptions, the official dignity of the Suffering One is a common feature. But it is remarkable that in one case (in Mark), the inscription is *confined* to this. There is nothing else, neither name or pronoun. We have only the marked distinction " *The King of the Jews.*" And looking back at the career of our Lord as recited in Mark, the hiding of Himself that there characterises Him, except as His ministry amidst sin and sorrow drew Him forth, how harmonious with the picture is this last touch of the Spirit!

Then as to the *diversity* that is observable. In Matthew and Luke alone, have we the demonstrative pronoun and the verb: " This is the King of the Jews," referring us back, as it were, for the appreciation of Him thus designated, to His portraiture in these Gospels, respectively. Accordingly we may read the pronoun " this," as emphasizing each portraiture that precedes; and predicate concerning the successive features of it as they are disclosed, " *This* is the King of the Jews." For example, (Matthew's)—This child born, and plotted against—This son called out of Egypt —This subject of so many prophecies fulfilled in Him—This benignant one—This Healer—This Saviour—This raiser of the dead in Israel—This Teacher—This Son of David and seed of Abraham —" IS THE KING OF THE JEWS."

Again, (Luke's)—This seed of the woman—This Son of Man—This Redeemer of the whole human family—This social one—This exhibitor of every moral beauty—This interpreter of God to man, and of man to himself, showing that he was made for God, the end of his being—This second Adam, in whom all mankind are interested—" IS THE KING OF THE JEWS."

But while the inscriptions in these Gospels,

Matthew and Luke, thus differ from that in Mark, they also differ from each other in this respect, that in Matthew the demonstrative pronoun has annexed to it, the personal name of our Lord, " *Jesus*," omitted in Luke—(" This is Jesus, the King of the Jews,") which, (like Joshua, the Hebrew form of the word,) having its root in the Divine name Jehovah, the covenant God of Israel, introduces another specification into his (Matthew's) inscription, as though he had written, " This King of the Jews was the Lord (Jehovah) of old, who brought Israel out of Egypt, who went before them, gave them bread from heaven, and water out of the rock; who healed them, their JEHOVAH JIREH—their JEHOVAH NISSI—their JEHOVAH ROPHI ; and it is remarkable that in the very style of narrative employed, a unity obtains between the recital of Jehovah's wonders in the Old Testament, and that of the miracles of our Lord, in Matthew.

Lastly, in John's Gospel, the inscription has a further peculiarity. The official relation " *King of the Jews*," is here, as also the personal name, " *Jesus*," but it is associated with " Nazareth," " JESUS OF NAZARETH, THE KING OF THE JEWS," plainly in keeping with the characteristic of Him in this Gospel, as *the rejected one from the commencement*. For, it is remarkable, that whereas the other Evangelists bring out that rejection only at the close of their histories, John introduces it in his first chapter, and in connexion with the transcendant glories of the rejected one : " He was in the world, and the world was made by Him, and the world knew Him not. He came unto His own, and His own received Him not." In the sequel, moreover, of this same chapter in John, occurs once and again the designation, "Jesus of Nazareth," at the hearing of which, even a Nathanael exclaims, " Can any good thing come out of Nazareth." (John i. 10, 11, 46, 47.)

Thus, for every variety in the Divine record of the words before us, there is a reason ; and to be insensible to that variety, much more to efface it, is to slight the wisdom of the Author, the Holy Ghost.

Indeed, in Scripture, (and it is only a corollary from its plenary, verbal, inspiration,) every variety of expression, how apparently soever insignificant, has an end to answer. There is nothing redundant or waste in nature, and the continuous discoveries of men of science evidence this—the very sea-weed, (the " *vilis alga* " of the Romans,) being now known to possess a most therapeutic property. And so it is, only in a superior degree, with the Word of God, which He has magnified above all His name. Nor can we doubt that the more that Word is studied in faith and humility, the more will this analogy become confirmed.*

* "The painter by the most delicate strokes of his brush, the musician by the swiftest touch of fleeting notes, exer-

Christian. I do trust that under God this line of remark has opened up a rich vein of truth for my study. It is certainly very suggestive. I suppose the variations in the accounts given of the scene of the Transfiguration, admit of the same sort of discrimination.

Pastor. Yes, and I think the key we have already used, has only to be applied to them, to evidence this.

Thus, as in the inscriptions over the cross, " THE KING OF THE JEWS" is the common term ; here it is " THE KINGDOM." But in Matthew, characterized by the Lion, (emblem of the Royalty of Messiah,) the introductory announcement is, " The Son of Man coming in His kingdom." (Matt. xvi. 28.)

In Mark, (the Ox, the symbol,) the words are simply, " The kingdom of God come with power." (Mark ix. 1.) Such the development of the ministry of Him, who in this Gospel was content to shine unseen of men.

In Luke, (the Man, the symbol,) we have, " the kingdom of God," a wider expression than that in Matthew. Even as the genealogy here ascends

cises the highest skill of his art ; and in the perfection of anything whatever, those minute particulars which escape the ears and eyes of the ignorant and unrefined, bestow the most exquisite delight on those who are capable of appreciating them,—a delight springing from the very root and essence of the thing itself. Such is the case with Holy Scripture."—*Bengel's Gnomon,* vol. i., p. 49.

higher than there, and indicates the dominion pourtrayed to be that of the second Adam, the executive of God in the domain of the whole earth.

Once more, in John, (the Eagle, the symbol,) where the personal glory set forth is that which issues from our Lord's essentially Divine relation, it is summarily contemplated as " the glory of the only begotten son of the Father." And no formal reference to the scene of the transfiguration is found in this Gospel—the very omission of this being as significant here, as its introduction in the other Gospels.

All this shading and distinguishing may appear to some minds, merely curious; and indeed, I reflect that my application of the key may be unskilful. But it is good to examine and search the Scriptures, and if we only have faith in them as the Word of God, we shall not hesitate thus to employ every power of microscope we possess.*

---

* " Some appear to disparage the style of Scripture, as barbarous. Some apologize for it, as the work of illiterate and unlearned men. Surely these notions are false and dangerous. The diction of Scripture, it is true, is not the language of any other composition in the world. The Greek of the New Testament is not the Greek of Xenophon, Plato or Demosthenes. It is a language of its own. And we need not scruple to affirm, that in precision of expression, in pure and native simplicity, in delicacy of handling, in the grouping of words and phrases, in dignified and majestic sublimity, it has no rival in the world. The more carefully it is studied, the more clearly will this appear. 'Nihil

What one discovers not, another may. We have now, (of some standing also,) a British Association for investigating science. Would that we had a similar association amongst Christians for the investigation of the Word of God! Indeed this ought to be one aspect of the Church of God, each generation of which, with its accumulation of scriptural knowledge, ought to be a pedestal for those succeeding, whereon to stand and enjoy a wider horizon of God's Revelation.

Christian. But how can such investigation be really pursued, as long as every word of the **sacred** volume is not regarded as inspired? I have no doubt that in what you have said, you have touched the root of the little proficiency made in Bible knowledge since the era of the Reformation. Since then, with some few exceptions, has not our progress been in. systematizing the acquisitions of our Reformers, rather than in

otiosum in sacra Scriptura' (Origen). Every sentence—we might almost say, every phrase—is fraught with meaning. As it is in the Book of Nature, so it is in the pages of· Holy Writ. Both are from the same Divine Hand. And if we apply to the language of Holy Scripture, the same microscopic process which we use in scrutinizing the beauties of the natural world, and which reveals to us exquisite colours and the most graceful texture in the petals of a flower, the fibres of a plant, the plumage of a bird, or the wings of an insect, we shall discover new sources of delight and admiration in the least portions of Holy Writ."—*Rev. Canon Wordsworth.*

adding to them, digging from the precious mine ourselves?

Pastor. Yes, and the systematizing being from inadequate, fragmentary knowledge, it has proved a hindrance very generally to the reception of fresh discoveries of truth when produced. Theology, in fact, instead of promoting, has thus obstructed progress. Instead of being, as Lord Bacon says of Natural Philosophy, *"ascendant and descendant from experiments to axioms, and from axioms to new discoveries,"* it has, on the contrary, as the same noble writer says of some of the established theories of his day, raised " fatal columns," beyond which students have feared to penetrate, though it was a promised land which lay before them. Their theology, alas! has been with many, a substitute for the Word of God, and not the auxiliary for interpreting it. As has been affirmed, by a modern Author of singular power, of a vicious school of painting, the mischief in Theology has been " man taking upon himself to modify God's work at his pleasure, and casting the shadow of himself on all he sees, constituting himself arbiter where it is his honour to be a disciple, and exhibiting his ingenuity by the attainment of combinations whose highest praise is, that they are impossible."*

Christian. A very forcible exposure indeed, of

* Ruskin, Preface to second edition of " Modern Painters," p. xxxiv.

the conventionalisms of our day in theological disquisitions. But may we not hope that the method of induction now pursued by our scientific men, will operate beneficially upon Christian students of revelation, in leading to reverent investigation of their field of knowledge.

Pastor. I trust that such indeed will be the case, and that the Bible will be studied, *not " as any other book,"* (i.e., as a human work,) which is the modern prescription, but as all God's works around us are studied, the student interrogating the sacred text, and sitting loose meanwhile to all traditions of men. Our most successful philosophers, it is remarkable, have been distinguished by this submissive spirit. Of Sir Isaac Newton it is recorded, that when Bradley and others observed a certain nutation of the earth which they could not account for, and were thinking it destroyed entirely the Newtonian system, they were under the greatest difficulty how to break it to Sir Isaac, and so proceeded to do it by degrees in the softest manner. But what was Sir Isaac's only answer ? " It may be so ; there is no arguing against facts and experiments."[*]

Christian. But is it not also to be apprehended that one mischief of the late " free handling," as it has been termed, of the most precious verities of the faith, may cause many, by way of cultivating sobriety of spirit, to recoil from investigation ?

* Rigaud's Life of Bradley, p. 62.

Pastor. There must be a tendency to this in some minds; and nothing, we may be sure, will more please our modern gainsayers, than Christians leaving to them the sphere of investigation. They want, indeed, to relegate religion to the region of faith altogether, and will not disturb us here, they say, if we allow them to rationalize on the subject according to their bent. In this line, they want to work on without molestation, and we shall have from them the fool's pardon for what we may adhere to of the old belief! The overture to this has been made in a variety of propositions. Thus we read in the " Essays and Reviews," that " what is not a subject for a problem, (and the miracles of the Gospel are put under this head,) may hold its place in a creed ;" * and a distinction is maintained between matters of knowledge and matters of faith; and it is affirmed as " generally admitted, that many points of important religious instruction, even conveyed under the form of fiction, (as in the instances of doctrines inculcated through parables,) are more congenial to the spirit of faith, than [any relations of historical events could be."† The drift of all this follows : " Miraculous narratives become invested with the character of articles of faith, if they be accepted in a less positive and certain light, as requiring some suspension of judgment as to their nature and cir-

* " Essays and Reviews," p. 127.
† *Ibid.*, pp. 126, 128.

D

cumstances, or perhaps as involving more or less of the parabolic or mythic character; or at any rate as received in connexion with, and for the sake of the doctrine inculcated." *

Now the proper answer to this is, that our faith (the Christian's faith) rests on knowledge communicated by God, knowledge of what He is, and of what He hath wrought for His name's sake. "We *know*" Him, therefore we trust in Him—"we *believe*," and therefore speak. "The grace of God. . . . *teaches* us." We are "*made wise* unto salvation." We *judge*. These propositions betoken intelligence, so that in attaining to them we renounce not reason, but *employ* it aright. It is the eye by which we use the telescope of faith; nor shall we put out the natural organ, as in pretended zeal for the instrument, these rationalists would have us to do; but we will exercise it with increased diligence. Only, let us remember, that to *confide*, belongs as much to the constitution of our being as to ratiocinate, and "through faith we understand." (Heb. xi. 2.)

And this brings me to observe—the fit winding up, perhaps, for our conversation—that the Word of God must be honoured by those who come to it, if they would receive light from it. Let us not forget, when we approach to judge it, it is all the while judging us, discerning the thoughts and intents of our heart. The *Personal*

* *Ibid.*, p. 142.

Word, our blessed Lord, when He was upon earth " committed Himself not" to certain who are said to have believed on Him, because " He knew what was in man." (John ii. 24, 25.) The *Written* Word will deal with us similarly. " Whosoever hath, to him shall be given ; and whosoever hath not, from him shall be taken even that which he seemeth to have." (Luke viii. 18.) He shall be left to stumble, · and shall be unmasked of his *seeming* reverence for the Divine oracles. Instances of such an issue to scepticism in all ages, might be adduced. Therefore let sceptics beware, and let us all remember the submission to the Word of God that becomes us—submission of mind to its mysteries—submission of heart to its doctrines—submission of the life to its precepts.

Christian. I trust, through God's mercy, that our conversation on the subject has deepened this spirit of submission in me. Nor shall I fear now in standing up for the maintenance of the fullest inspiration of my precious Bible.

I see that it is before the age in every thing, pregnant with answers to meet every cavil. Would that the assaults made on it, only led our learned men to show their faith in it, by developing its internal evidences, letting it speak for itself, and renouncing all apologetic tone. Israel of old, in steadying the Ark in *their* way only provoked God ; whereas had they simply carried it as pre-scribed, all had been well. We can imagine a natural flower pronounced to be artificial, but surely the best mode of vindicating it as the work of God, would be to apply the lens and show forth its structure and organization. And is not the structure and organization of the Bible, with its component parts, produced at intervals of centuries and even millennaries, all fitting together in a wonderful unity, the best demonstration of its Divine Authorship?

Pastor. I thoroughly go with you in this view, and rejoice to see that, in spite of many anomalies which traditional interpretation of various portions of Scripture has put in the way, the marvellous unity of the whole has commended itself to our Theologians. Bengel, for example, thus writes: "Not only are the various writings, when considered separately, worthy of God, but also when received as a whole, they exhibit one entire and perfect body, unencumbered by excess, unimpaired by defect."* Again, "The Old Testament comprises thirty-nine books, (counting the Book of Lamentations separately,) while the New Testament contains twenty-seven separate writings —yet, from the unity of spirit pervading this vast literary collection, they constitute, really, only one book—a second intellectual creation (Ps. xix)." †

Once more, "From the idea of the Canon

* Bengel's "Gnomon," vol. i., pp. 5, 6.
† Lange's Commentary on St. Matthew's Gospel, vol. i., p. 20.

flows the necessary assumption that all the portions composing it are bound together by a common principle into one whole, and this is the. religious element peculiar to Hebraism, which runs through it like a thread from beginning to end of the Divine revelation."*

All this is cheering. But yet these writers have not discerned the composite unity of the wondrous volume in one of its most exquisite displays. I allude to their amalgamating in one homogeneous sphere of import, the Gospels, Acts, Epistles and Apocalypse, instead of eliminating the Epistles, as belonging to the great central device of Eternal Wisdom, and leaving the rest to fill up the circle of Old Testament Prophecy.

Christian. Do you mean that the Gospels, Acts, and Apocalypse, relate to a different subject from the Epistles?

Pastor. Yes, that subject being, respectively, the kingdom *presented* (the Gospels)—the kingdom *rejected* (the Acts)—and at length, the kingdom *established* amidst overwhelming judgments upon its enemies (the Apocalypse). Thus the Judaism, as it may be .called, of the Old Testament, is yet to find its development in Christianity, i.e., the sufferings of Christ (penitently believed in by Jew and Gentile, nationally), and His kingdom and power and glory. Meanwhile the present dispensation—the Divine

* Havernach's Introduction to the Old Testament, p. 386.

parenthesis in God's dealings with the Jews, (and the Gentiles subordinately to them,)—is yielding its special fruits in the development of THE CHURCH, wherein is no subordination, but both Jew and Gentile are " one in Christ." In other words, out of the simple Personal Christ of the Old Testament, is being now evolved, the complex or mystical Christ of the New—the Head and the members. (1 Cor. xii. 12.) That there should be this complexity, was indeed the eternal purpose of God ; and so the Church, the members of Christ, are distinctly declared to have been " chosen in Him," their Head " before the foundation of the world." (Eph. i. 4.) But, in the wisdom of God, the occasion for the evolution of this " Mystery," only arrived when the Personal Christ was rejected of His own people—the Jews. Nor did the reservation of it entirely cease, till that rejection was consummated by resistance to the oft-repeated testimony of the Holy Ghost, by Peter, by Stephen, and at last by Paul—the ordained Apostle of the new dispensation.

Christian. If I understand you aright, then, you consider the normal subject of Divine Revelation from the call of Abraham onward, to be the salvation and government of mankind ; and that the Epistles belong to the *episode* which is now being transacted in the calling of THE CHURCH —a new phase of Redemption, and not to be confounded with the other ?

Pastor. Precisely so. The *salvation* of men (Jews and Gentiles) flows from our blessed Lord as the seed of Abraham; their *government*, and that of the whole earth, from his relationships " Son of David" and " Son of Man." But the eternal glory of the Church flows from His prior relation of Head, and " appointed heir of all things." Throughout Old Testament Prophecy, and even throughout the Gospels, except in latent type, the Church is hidden in the Person of Messiah, like as Eve at the creation of the human race was hidden in the constitution of Adam. At length, as a separate existence was given to Eve from the opened side of Adam, so now from the risen and ascended Christ—the second Adam—is being developed by the Holy Ghost, the Church of this dispensation, a special election of grace, so intimately united to Him, that they are denominated " members of His body, of His flesh, and of His bones." (Ephesians v. 30.)

Christian. But do we not read of " the blessing of Abraham coming on the Gentiles through Jesus Christ." (Gal. iii. 14.) And is not the reference here to Gentiles called under the present dispensation ?

Pastor. Admitting this—and that the common benefit of salvation by *grace*, (the characteristic of the Divine Covenant with Abraham,) is thus derived to the Jews, the Gentiles, and the Church of God, what forbids that accompanying that salvation, a special intimacy of union with the seed of Abraham, (the Messiah,) together with its corresponding glory, should accrue to some—even the Church—from that Messiah's further relationship to them? " Salvation," *all* salvation,—the salvation of mankind, " is of the Jews," through Him who is emphatically "the seed of Abraham." But this is quite consistent with such salvation being unto varieties of glory, according to the manifold glories that belong to Him.

In the family, there is a participation by all—wife, children, and servants, in the protection of the Head of the family. But to the wife, because he is her husband, and to the children, because he is their father, belongs more than protection. So to the family of the Redeemed, accrues salvation, from the penalty and power of sin, and through the same precious blood of the cross ; but by virtue of their various relationships, through grace, to the Person of the Redeemer, they possess various dignities and prerogatives. In some places, the Spirit of God has in view the grand pervading unity ; in others, the distinguishing variety, and we ought to appreciate both. But, query, is not this latter too much lost sight of ; whilst yet herein lies the spring and power of our spiritual life, that on which the Holy Ghost, the Comforter, especially acts. Thus, to cite one example, the prayer of the Apostle is that we " may know what is the hope of His calling, and what the riches of the glory of His inheritance in the saints." (Eph. i. 18.) Here the apprehension of our calling and His glory is connected, the one with the other ; and endowed with the riches of the glory which flow from Himself, He glories in us as His inheritance. Just as He prays also in John xvii. But this is getting into another subject than Inspiration, and upon which my views, such as they are, are already in print,* and so I abstain. I feel also that to merely suggest a point of truth is frequently better than dilation on it ; especially, when in order to its due reception, it has to be learned from the Word of God.

With one or two closing remarks, then, I finish this conversation. Let us prove every thing by the Word of God. Mariners of old, when they discovered the properties of the loadstone, no longer coasted by observation, but trusting to their new acquisition, committed themselves boldly to the deep. Let us act similarly by our Heavenly compass, and evince, practically, our conviction that " every word of God is pure ;" helping one another by investigation, the lame man mounting upon the shoulders of the blind man, each contributing in his measure to the discovery of precious truth.

And let us beware of resting in the attainments of those who have gone before us.

* " The Eternal Purpose of God." London : Nisbet and Co.

"I charge you before God and the blessed Angels," said Robinson, in his address to the Pilgrim fathers as they embarked on board the *Mayflower*, " that you follow me no further than you have seen me follow the Lord Jesus Christ. The Lord has more truth yet to break forth out of His Holy word. I cannot sufficiently bewail the condition of the Reformed Churches who are come to a period in religion, and will go at present no further than the instruments of their Reformation. Luther and Calvin were great and shining lights in their times, yet they penetrated not into the counsel of God. I beseech you remember it—it is an article of your faith—that you be ready to receive whatever truth shall be made known to you from the written Word of God."

What is this but an exposition of the Apostle's threefold precept. " Despise not prophecyings, prove all things, hold fast that which is good." (1 Thess. v. 20, 21.) May this be the issue of all the ferment which is going on around us in regard to Divine truth!

Printed at the Operative Jewish Converts' Institution, Palestine Place, Bethnal Green, N.E.

WORKS

REV. JAMES KELLY, M.A.

PUBLISHED BY

NISBET AND CO., LONDON.

I.

Fourth Edition, price Four Shillings.

THE ETERNAL PURPOSE OF GOD;

LECTURES ON SUBJECTS CONNECTED WITH PROPHECY.

" We are not surprised that this work has reached a fourth edition. It is one of the freshest, richest, and most thoughtful volumes on prophecy which we have ever read."—*The Quarterly Journal of Prophecy.*

" I have read your book with much interest. The title scarcely conveys an adequate description of the contents, as you have not only entered into the subject of prophecy, but attempted the mighty task of calling the attention of the Church to what our older divines call the 'supercreation grace of God,' and demonstrating that creation as truly as redemption, though in a different sense, requires a Mediator."—*Rev. H. M'Neile, D.D.*

" There is much that is really able and ingenious in this work; much that is original and fresh in thought and exposition."—*Presbyterian Review.*

" Marked by a deep study of Scripture, and cannot fail of suggesting to the reader many interesting trains of thought."—*Christian Ladies' Magazine.*

" They are well worthy an attentive study."—*The Prophetic Herald.*

" This treatise is already well known, and we shall do little more than notice its appearance in a fourth edition. It might be classed among works on prophecy, but it far more deserves to be considered as a treatise on that deep subject,—the purpose or counsel of God in all his works. And no one can come in contact with its massive generalising thought without receiving a stimulus from it. Whether one assents to Mr. Kelly's prophetic views or dissents from them, he will be struck with his views of the self-manifestation of God in all His works."—*The British and Foreign Evangelical Review.*

" The practical portions of the book, and the hearty exhortations with which even the most speculative and argumentative chapters of it are concluded, will commend themselves to the judgment and the conscience of every Christian.........The absence of dogmatism, however, and the knowledge of, and love for the Scriptures, of which every page gives evidence, will make the work welcome to all who take any deep interest in the study of prophecy."—*Freeman.*

"We can only express our admiration of the learning he displays in every page, and yet the unostentatious modesty—the true sign of distinguished merit—by which his discussions are everywhere characterized."—*Scottish Press.*

"There is much valuable matter......the volume is well deserving o' attention; the principles, doctrines, and teaching are all trustworthy. We have much pleasure in recommending the book."—*Dublin Christian Examiner.*

"Contain truth far beyond what can be found in any of the curren works of the day."—*The Prospect.*

II.

THE APOCALYPSE INTERPRETED in the Light of "THE DAY OF THE LORD."

The First and Second Volumes now complete, price Six Shillings each.

THE TITLE indicates the principle on which the Work is being conducted and GOD IS CONSULTED AS HIS OWN HISTORIAN.

"Though in many things we differ from Mr. Kelly, we appreciate hi writings highly. They are spiritual, acute, clear, and full of vigorou thought. The close and careful comparison of Scripture with Scriptur which marks Mr. Kelly's writings, is always interesting, and often mo instructive. * *

"The leading idea of Mr. Kelly's exposition is, that all the events pr dicted in the Apocalypse are to take place *in the day of the Lord*, that i *after* the Lord has come and caught up His saints. The day of the Lor he says, 'means a time distinct from, and *posterior* to the coming of tl Lord, for the saints of this dispensation.' Many of the practical remarl are admirable."—*The Quarterly Journal of Prophecy.*

"In general, clear views of the position and hope of the Church, indispensable to all progress in understanding the Revelation."—*T. Prospect.*

Vol. III. is preparing for the press.

III.

Price One Shilling.

APOCALYPTIC INTERPRETATION; OR, THE APOCALYPS INTELLIGIBLE,

Not in any History of the Past, as alleged by the Rev. E. B. ELLIOTT, but

IN THE LIGHT OF "THE DAY WHEN THE SON OF MA IS REVEALED."

"Successful in exposing the unsoundness of Mr. Elliott's theory... The general principle that the prophetic portion of the Revelation is) unfulfilled and will receive its accomplishment *after* the ascension of t Church to meet the Lord in the air, is asserted with much distinctne and illustrated by various arguments and analogies founded on t testimony of Scripture."—*The Prospect.*

X.

Price Twopence.

THE TABERNACLE A WITNESS FOR GOD.

XI.

Price Twopence.

SPEECH AT A PUBLIC MEETING AT YORK, AGAINST THE ENDOWMENT OF MAYNOOTH.

XII.

Price One Shilling and Sixpence. Second Edition.

PSALMS AND HYMNS.

Selected and Revised for Public Worship, (with several original.)

XIII.

Price Sixpence.

JEWISH HOPE,

WITH ITS CONCOMITANT EVENTS, THE KEY TO THE PROPHETIC PARABLES

Illustrated by the Exposition of the Parable of the Tares.

XIV.

Price Sixpence.

"AVENGE ME OF MINE ADVERSARY,"

NOT THE CRY OF THE CHURCH OF GOD.

Being an Exposition of the Parable of the Importunate Widow, (Luke xviii. 1—8,) with Remarks on the Imprecatory Psalms.

XV.

GOSPEL TRACTS.

I. God our Saviour.   II. Do you love Jesus?
III. Salvation now—God's Gift.

London : NISBET and Co., Berners Street.